Also by K. L. Cook

Last Call

The Girl from Charnelle

Love Songs for the Quarantined

Marrying Kind

The Art of Disobedience

Lost Soliloquies

Poems

K. L. Cook

Ice Cube Press, LLC
North Liberty, Iowa, USA

Lost Soliloquies

First Edition

ISBN 9781948509121

Library of Congress Control Number: On file

Ice Cube Press, LLC (Est. 1991)
205 N. Front Street
North Liberty, Iowa 52317 USA
www.icecubepress.com | steve@icecubepress.com

The paper used in this publication meets the minimum requirements of the American National Standard for Information Sciences—Permanence of Paper for Printed Library Materials, ANSI Z39.48-1992.

Manufactured in USA

Author photo: Lena Menefee-Cook
Cover design: Lena Menefee-Cook and Charissa Menefee

For Charissa

Lost Soliloquies

And in Life's noisiest hour,
There whispers still the ceaseless Love of Thee,
The heart's Self-solace and soliloquy.

— Coleridge, "The Presence of Love"

And when I love thee not, Chaos is come again.

— Othello

Reading the Signs

for Sheila

I wonder if you're still
in Vietnam and Cambodia,
sweating muchly and fending
off the mice that playeth
about thy feet.

We've traveled as well, to Boston
for nine days to visit our son
and to trample over
the stones of American history
in search of fresh lemonade.

Then we crossed the border
at Niagara Falls,
with its shoddy neon splendor,
to the Stratford Festival in Ontario,
where we saw
some disappointing Shakespeare
and a great Mother Courage.

Now we're back in Iowa,
where the thunderstorms
and tornado warnings
cry havoc
and visitors descend on us.

Everywhere I turn there are
teenage girls giggling and shrieking,
but the house is big enough
that I can find quieter crannies
in which to curl up with books
while I await the muse,
which has come thus far
in the form of odd profundities,
half-baked theories,
lost soliloquies,
and promises of greater fluency—

assuming I'm reading the signs rightly
and not just hopefully.

Exit Strategies

Exit Strategies

Tragedy is the ending-obsessed genre.
The dying fall, catharsis and elegy,
stages littered with bodies.
Shakespeare's best end bloody
in gloriously colossal waste.
Richard the Hunchback pleading for a horse.
Romeo and Juliet poisoned and daggered
in the Capulet tomb, the Friar fleeing the scene.
The fratricide, suicide, fatal chalice,
and stabbings of Denmark's royal court.
The storm systems, eye-gouging, hangings,
and howls of Lear's bleak realm.
The bed stacked with Othello and the
dead wives, Iago militantly mute.
Antony's shame, Cleopatra's asps.
Macbeth's head pinned to a pike.
Nobody left to exeunt.

Her First Husband

Lady Macbeth: I have given suck, and know
How tender 'tis to love the babe that milks me.

Macbeth: Upon my head they plac'd a fruitless crown
And put a barren scepter in my grip.

He came to me himself and told me that
he loved my wife and wanted to marry her.
He wanted my permission and needed
me to annul her, to risk disgrace,
so that he could achieve his ambition.
He spoke without fear of retribution
(I could not hurt him),
but with courtesy and respect
for my predicament and appropriate
shame for his betrayal.

They had been lovers for months
before he approached me. I had, in my
way, arranged the courtship. He had not
exactly been my friend, nor would I have
wanted a friend for this charge. But we had
been together in the field and did not,
from my vantage point, harbor
animosity toward one another.

I could tell, from the first time I saw them
together, they were meant for each other.
She would do him good, would uncover

what lay hidden, would blow on any spark
of genius, would nurture what must be
nurtured and root out what impediments
remained. She was a natural teacher,
if a stern and exacting one.

Honestly, I could never really satisfy her,
certainly not since my injury.
There was an insatiability about her
that frightened and enthralled me.
There were times, in our years together,
when I believed her spirit would be
dampened by our marriage.

Yes, it is true we had children—
three boys, all dead by age seven,
the eldest before his first year passed.
She loved our sons, took seriously
her role as tutor and molder
of their characters, was grief-stricken,
though her grief frightened me.
A carapace developed around her,
hardening with each fresh tragedy.

It is strange that I have outlived her.
There was something mysteriously
perennial about her—as if she had
emerged from a planetary
substance and was capable, if she
applied herself to it, of invulnerability.
But no one remains invulnerable.

I have remarried—a young, docile wife,
naturally gracious, kinder, less hungry
in her appetites. This suits me better,
I have told myself many times,
especially when the full extent
of the tyranny and horror were revealed.
My first wife's suicide.
Her second husband's head fastened,
rightly so, to the end of a pike.

I should feel privileged, blessed, fortunate,
lucky. And I am fortunate with the trade
I made in wives. But I still dream
of her, my first wife. It is not uncommon,
I know, for aging men who have lived
multiple lives to carry in their wake
the history of younger, fiercer loves.

I dream about when we were happiest,
after our first son was born. I remember,
months later, the child in the cradle
beside our bed, swaddled in the softest wool,
sheared from a lamb on my estate.
The child waking in the middle of the night
to the sounds of our lovemaking,
our first encounter since his birth.

And my wife—my first wife—bringing him
to our bed, holding him close to her breast.
I wrapped them both inside my arms,
studied them, the moon streaming through

the rain-smeared window, as she rubbed
her nipple over his smiling gums,
teasing him, coaxing him, the three
of us there, naked beneath the blankets.

We watched our son, who would be dead
within two months, taken by the mysterious
plague that killed most of our hamlet
that spring, watched him smile and then greedily
fill himself, the thin milk from my wife's breast
oozing from the side of his contented mouth.

Zachary Does Not Apologize—East Texas 1933

Before the accident, I was a rutting pig.
Domestic life didn't suit me. I believed
myself destined for greater things.

This was the problem with being born
in a place like this, in a life like this,
and then to make the choices you make,
with a wife and too many children,
and a son that dies, and a farm to tend,
and that wife hardened by grief.
You try in vain to keep
the world together without
any money and too much dust.

But what can you do when you have failed?
You do not want to work this hard anymore.
What is the use?

You look around you, at your own family
and your wife's family and the neighbors
on all these ramshackle farms and ranches,
and you see nothing but constant struggle
against an inconstant god and fickle weather
and a fate indifferent to your misery.

So yes, you look elsewhere.
And the women appear, as if summoned.

The Son's Lament

Perhaps the son of every father
who dies before middle age
feels as if he has been robbed
of something that should be his,
and what is left, as in every theft,
is palpable vacancy, a hole
where a whole once was
and now more valued because
of its absence. Mourning, in the guise
of anger or bewilderment, elevates
the stolen man. My father's death is
a defining event I know will reverberate
for the rest of my life: a clock with bells
that chime off-key, and frequently.

First Fall—October 1945

Why is he on the roof, and how
did he get there? Four and a half
years old. October but an Oklahoma
Indian summer—brutal, searing,

the green and white shingles
of his grandmother's farmhouse
scalding his bare soles, the seat
of his pants, his palms.

He grasps the spinning silver turret,
studies the blisters as they rise on
his fingers. A crow lands on the roof,
inches from his face, stares, one eye

punctured. He extends his blistered
finger to the bird, who determines
the relative worth of his appendage,
then flutters its scraggly wings.

The feathers shadow and confuse him.
His feet burn. Down the slope
of the roof he goes. He should grab
the attic ledge, but doesn't,

looks instead at the faint white sun above.
The air, so hot, shivers as the ragged
gutter slits the inner crook of his
elbow, right where Granny pinches.

He somersaults past the kitchen's
white lace curtains, where he glimpses
his mother sorting quilt scraps—purple,
red, and orange. The porch railing

rises to him, a splintered truth
he's not ready to absorb.
He hears before he feels it punch him.
Flesh, muscle, bone bend in, then back out:

the miracle he will swear by for decades.
The grass, surprisingly cool, smells
of dew and sun-baked cow patties left
by Imogen, who wanders the farm like

a pet when not being milked.
Close to his eye, a ladybug climbs
a green blade, traverses the bridge
of his nose, squats on his eyelash.

She skitters down his cheek,
across his cracked lips,
then leaps from his chin
and is gone.

A fall and a kiss,
a kiss and a fall:
this will be the story
of my father's life.

First Fool—April 1946

During their afternoon naps,
his mother allows him to lay
his head against the swell of
her stomach, sometimes pliant,
sometimes hard and ridged
like an enormous walnut.

As she sleeps, he traces blue
and red paisleys on her dress,
cups his ear against the soft hill
of her body and listens to what
his father calls the constant
whoosh of digestive acid.

He waits for the creature inside
to whisper a secret to him, and
finally, on the first day of April,
a knob of elbow or knee presses
against his ear, a code, he thinks,
a signal. SOS. Mayday.

Then his mother's stomach fists.
The bed's suddenly drenched.
His mother whimpers, clutches his
hand so hard the fingertips redden.
He grits his teeth until she releases
her hold on him and opens her eyes.

Later, in the parlor with his three aunts,
he feels guilty about wanting sleep
and wishes his mother would not
scream. His father stands by the closed
bedroom door, cigarette after cigarette
after cigarette shrinking into gray ash.

Just after midnight, he hears a new voice,
a stammering, chirping cough. Granny
cracks the door. Aunt June hoists him
to her hip, and he nestles his head into
the crook of her neck, watches the last
embers of the fire flicker and wither.

His aunt glides to his parents' door,
sets him down, and he wobbles
to the bed, toward his father's gap-
toothed grin. Inside a white blanket,
pressed against his mother's chest,
is the creature he's been waiting for.

He climbs atop the bed to see a face,
purple and wrinkly, gooey half-
opened eyes. A disappointment.
Good thing he waited until
after midnight to come, his father jokes.
He feels foolish for not getting it.

Hail Mary

My grandmother's third husband towered
above the rest of the family, a tall, gaunt,
gray-complexioned specter, an insurance
salesman with a wrinkly neck, a widow's
peak, and a penchant for plaid shirts.
I remember little about him, other than
his cheerfully somber presence in Childress.

This was 1975. I was eleven. My family
had driven to the Texas Panhandle
for the holidays, and we stayed with Ed
and my grandmother. A family reunion,
a snowy day, the Roger Staubach-led Cowboys
in the playoffs—the miraculous Hail Mary
pass to Drew Pearson, vaulting the Cowboys
past the Vikings and eventually
into the Super Bowl, where they lost,
in a heartbreaker, to the Pittsburgh Steelers.

Big Ed, amused by our histrionic enthusiasm
for the game, felt our elation disproportionate
to the event. Later that spring, Ed put
a gun to his head and blew his brains out.
My grandmother never married again.

Trampoline

For a dollar an hour,
we'd jump on a trampoline
at Bobby's, the kid with
muscular dystrophy down
the street who found a good
way to make money
and friends, and keep
the neighborhood kids
in his debt and good graces.

For him, we did somersaults,
wrestled with one another,
flipped and butt-bounced,
levitated high above
the backyard fence,
where we could see
the business of the suburbs—
lawns edged, mowers
towing their sweaty owners,
sprinklers arcing silver,
cars in a redemptive lather—
all the while watching
Bobby in his motorized
wheelchair, his head held upright
in a steel brace, his noodly legs
dangling into enormous
white tennis shoes, glistening
from no use, no scuffs.

Bobby teased our incompetence,
egging on competitions,
smirking and cackling
at our near-quadriplegic
tumbles to the concrete moat
surrounding his trampoline,
until his mother wheeled him in
for his iron lung treatment,
where we could see, through
the sliding glass door, a boy
trapped in a silver tube,
the rest of us leaping
in the reflection.

DREAMING OF ROY ORBISON

My father died years ago in Las Vegas,
but, too pregnant, I didn't go to the funeral.
In the strange time after the birth, I kept
dreaming of Roy Orbison. He would take my
hand in his, and I'd be surprised by his
soft, pink palms, the guitar-calloused fingertips.

Each night he escorted me to
the top of a hill and sang:
I'll be cry-yyyy-in' over you,
Cry-yyyy-in' over you,
Oh, what can I do-oo-oo?
It wasn't sad, just tender, high-pitched,
and each time, as his voice crescendoed,
I feared that it would crack, a ghost
sound already in my head, a glass shattering.

Only now, years later, my son living
with my ex-husband three hundred
and thirty-one miles away from me,
do I remember that my father loved
Roy Orbison, loved the strange
juxtaposition of that quivering falsetto,
the girlish sadness of those high-pitched
songs emerging from a man
who also wore black jeans, satin shirts,
slick hair, and dark sunglasses
that made you wonder if he was blind.

Clyde Barrow Axes His Big Toe

I remember finagling my way
into that ax, promising to be a
good old boy, someone to trust
with a cutting tool.

It served them right, thinking
they could trust any convict,
especially poor white trash
like me. If the tables had been
turned, I wouldn't trust me—
a wayward youth, that was for
damn sure, another boy manured
in poverty, rotting shame
a fact of life, the mother a saint
with no protective powers, no sirree.
She wasn't saving us from starving
half the goddamn time, and my father
wasn't doing a helluva lot better,
the ten of us living in that storage
room with Dr Pepper and Nehi signs.

I never wanted a soda pop after that.
I'd slept in that syrup, had inhaled
enough of its rancid stickiness—
the odor of Texas and hunger
and nobody giving a good goddamn—
the stink you know all too well
when you live with nine other people

in a sweet-smelling storage room
in the middle of summer.

I swore to myself I'd get the hell
out of that graveyard the first chance
I had. But three scrapes with the law
later, I was in Eastham prison, ready
to ax my big toe off because that might
speed up my sentence, and to get the ax,
I had to act like the good old boy
I couldn't be, would never be,
the kind my father was,
and where did it get him?
The poorhouse, that's where.
No sirree Bob.

One whack and it was done.
A sizzling pain—then throbbing
buffered by shock—and before
I knew it they gave me a shot
of morphine, gauzed my toe,
and then I was out of that skunkhole
in six months, and back with Buck
and the boys, and ready to show
them all, by God, you bet we would.

I vowed to stick their piggy noses in it.
Let them smell that shit.

Postcard from Frank Lloyd Wright's Chauncey Griggs House

My Dear Olgivanna,

Here's my latest. It's the light I love—
blue, melancholy dusk streaming
into the burnished room, like a cathedral
that emanates light from the natural world.

But I could never live here.
The long Northwestern nights lack the freezing
claw of the Midwest, that Puritan weather that
always makes me feel good for enduring, as if
I've earned the warmth of a hearth in every room,
the crackling heat that I can never get enough of.

And my past follows me to this cathedral, too.
I think of that man blocking the doorway in Taliesin—
the only doorway, my great folly—
scything everyone I love as they tried to escape.
If it weren't for those memories
and my love of hard winter,
I would stay here in the blue light of Tacoma.

Love, Frank

Pecans

I kneel under my grandmother's pecan tree,
dazzled by the tent worms performing
acrobatics on the third gnarled limb.
They will die soon.

The tree surgeon will be here Monday to burn
the limb and the whole silken ensemble.
But now, mesmerized as they wriggle
in their cotton candy nets, somersault
around rotten shells, vault over slender
twigs, wrap themselves like live Christmas
ribbons around one young green nut,
I pity them.

My eighth summer I hovered in this Oklahoma
house for two months while my parents
chewed their divorce papers. I tried to ignore
my grandparents and nursed my fury with Edgar
Rice Burroughs novels. Peeling the bark,
I found myself, ridiculous as it seemed,
apologizing to this tree.

I could not stand the way my widow-peaked
grandfather had me, each morning, fetch
him a bowl full of pecans from the backyard,
was driven mad as he splintered shell
after shell between the steel gums
of his nutcracker.

The tiny shards flew into the seat cushions,
the small slivers on the floor a personal affront,
my barefoot traipses treacherous.
I hated how he spent the day fingering
and chiseling the brown-white meat
from the cavities,
how he gobbled and chomped,
gobbled and chomped,
as if his life depended on it.

In June, I crept from my bed,
slipped beneath the gray warble of his snore,
and armed with flashlight and paper sacks,
I plucked the pecans from their backyard cemetery,
stowing them in a garden shed.
One night my grandmother appeared
on the back porch, the moths fluttering
in the neon light, fluttering
in the white cobweb of her hair.
Wordlessly, she gathered the shells
with me that night and for the rest of the
summer, while my grandfather, cursing
nut-thieving neighbors, bought packaged pecans
from Earl's Grocery Mart.

Now, as the calloused hand of a hot August breeze
passes through my hair and through the wormy silk
of the tree, I think of my grandfather, dead
after a missile broke from its chains, then
slid from an eighteen-wheeler's truck-bed,

and flipped his truck through the air
like a Tiddlywink.

I think of my great-grandmother rotting inside
a six-year coma, think of my blue-faced father
as a coronary squeezed the thick nut of his heart,
and my pregnant sister, her fetus withering
in the uterine shell.

Next week, like always, my grandmother will watch
The 700 Club, read her weekly *Gospel Advocate*,
bathe hunchbacked and moaning women in
the nursing home, where I refuse to go,
but where she, good soul that she is, soothes
with her laughter their broken pelvises, kidney failures,
tumors, and strokes.

Her answer is not my answer, but we are still here
together. I've seen, in her garden shed,
beyond a thicket of cobwebs, the decades-old sacks
of chambered nuts, black and rotten.
Tomorrow I'll drive off, leaving
my grandmother and the tent worms
to wait for Monday.

Little Deaths

Evening in October, but Indian summer had brought
a heat wave after weeks of cool autumn, and now
the days were muggy and warm, reminding me of Saigon,
with that dampness in the air that I so enjoyed,
mulched grass recalling rice paddies.

It was the first good memory I'd had of the war
since I'd returned, the first unalloyed memory.
My older brother barbecued brisket
and ribs for me and his cronies.
The sky a marbled blue and orange.

I sipped my third vodka tonic, awaiting the pleasant
pop that always seemed to arrive, like clockwork,
in the middle of the third drink, then a hum that would carry
me through the night, as if my body were a vibrato.
I always welcomed that moment.

I'd gotten good over the years at knowing when it
would arrive. I'd begun to yearn for those few seconds
before the pop, like the moment before an orgasm,
the moment that, as you get older, you want to prolong
because you know once you come, there is, as the poets say,

a little death. No going back. There was a pocket of silence
with all of us lost in this unexpectedly warm Dallas twilight,
closing our eyes. You don't see that moment often among men.
It's usually ruined by talk—about sports or music or sex—
the kind of silence I'd learned to relish

and even sought during my time in and after Vietnam.
In fact, the military is the place where you find this peace.
There is a lot of silence in war, more than you'd think.
It's often sinister, fraught with anxiety,
expectation, terror. But every once in a while,

usually after a long day of work that makes you feel
temporarily good about yourself and your service
to American history, you'd be privy to this silence.
Twilight evenings in the barracks, without the imminent
threat of shrapnel exploding unexpectedly in your face.

Men sitting quietly, drinking beers, smell of wild boar
roasting in a makeshift barbecue pit or over a campfire—
the sky also marbled, the booze working its lulling magic
on us all so that what we felt was the silence of fellowship.

A feeling I would long for my entire life.

Love Song for His Late Wife

How dark it must be there, where you are now,
black with the moonless quiet of the plains,
where there are no planes,
no honks or stolen screeches,
no sullen neighbors
with Mad Dog 20/20 and bad insulation,
tinfoil on the rabbit ears,
blankets and duct tape belted
to broken windows,
their underfed dogs bawling.

No firecrackers or skyrockets.
No puberty gangs courting the sirens.
No boom-box bravado.
No, it is quiet there,
where you are, and pitch.

I think of the way we made love,
in the years before the children,
two doors down from your parents,
each vacation day a deliciously slow tease,
a yearning for night and that bedroom
after the delay of cool breeze, swaying grass.

It was best when I'd slip into the room
an hour after you'd gone to bed,
after midnight, the house shut down,
hatches locked, and find your naked,

half-sleeping surprise beneath the blankets,
between the warming sheets.

I'd never known such darkness,
so thick I couldn't tell if my eyes were open.
The thin-walled cities can't afford
such black quiet, sight so obliterated
that other senses compensate:

two hundred watts of taste, smell, touch.
On nights like that, we were unleashed,
as if the hot sap had been rising all day,
preparing for a patient bursting.

We swam in darkness, just rhythm
and motion, black lake of flesh and hair,
warm waterfall of breast and thigh.
We navigated, in the sleepy moments,
with lip and tongue, with hand and nail,
the uncharted regions: the hinge of kneecap,
the ticklish ribs, the blades of spine,
the tender button of tailbone, warm suspense.

We waited for the white noise
of the air-conditioner so we could strike out
together, for the deep water, the full embrace,
accompanied by the aluminum rapids of the vents
and the splash of your father's snore.

How dark it must be there, where you are now,
black with the moonless quiet of the plains.

January at MacDowell

Even though the morning sun
is clouded with snow
this Tuesday in New Hampshire,
this place blinds and deceives;
a fresh coverlet ashes the branches
of the boughs, the pathways thick,
unblemished by tracks.

I could tumble through meadows,
leave my mark on the blank pages,
angel-wing and figure-eight,
create rounded men and women,
luminous sentinels
in the dark to greet fellow artists
on their midnight studio hikes.

I see it clearly, me molding a
glistening city, designing a world
of ice both friends and strangers
may believe is real, in the shadowy
twilight or moon-dusted dark,
and might even recognize as mine.

But yesterday, I stepped on a snow
mound and fell through to my thighs.
Drop-offs are blanketed in beauty,
like Old Testament temptation—
Delilah lulling Samson to sleep,

the sharpened blade beneath the pillow,
poor Eve meditating on the ripened
wonder of that tree, skinning
the lovely bark with her fingernails.

For all I know that meadow could be a lake.
A thin fracture in the ice, and I'd
plunge through with my thick boots,
my layers, the slack weight of my age.
I'd be a goner, dredged from the
bottom days later, or perhaps
in the first warm blossoming of spring.

And what would be my legacy?
A story in the back pages of a couple
of small-town newspapers:
Writer Plunges Through Ice and Drowns.
Perhaps a photo in the MacDowell newsletter.

No grand tragedy, my death,
no cause for national mourning.
A private sadness for those who loved me,
a headache for the maintenance crew,
a flurry of memos for colony administrators
haggling over the definition of negligence.

If I'm lucky I might become
a local joke, nestled smirks
in the bar at Grover's Corners,
the communal laughs of tipsy listeners.
Or perhaps a legend for future residents,

sipping wine, searching for the consoling
anecdotes and myths of colony lore
to ease them back toward billiards
or sleep, or maybe on wintry mornings
like this one, toward their work
and the ghosts of their own dead.

And really, it's not so bad to have my life
or anyone's life, for that matter,
compressed into the language of warning,
distilled into the haiku of a sign
nailed to a New Hampshire fence post:

Danger in Winter
Foolish Artists Please Beware
Lake Hidden Beneath

The Senator's Dream

Iago: Even now, now, very now, an old black ram
Is tupping your white ewe. Arise, arise . . .

Brabantio: This accident is not unlike my dream:
Belief of it oppresses me already.

Gratiano: Poor Desdemona! I am glad thy father's
dead: Thy match was mortal to him, and pure grief . . .

If I had known how things would end,
I would not have welcomed him as a peer
into my home as graciously as I did.
He bewitched me, as was his method.

In my dreams, my daughter sometimes
visited me, but on more than one occasion,
he was there too, insinuating himself
between us, his hands clutching

her shoulders, the raised callouses of his open
palm inviting her into his web. A celebrated
warrior maybe, but also a charlatan and a thief.
I should have known, but I did not respect

nor appreciate the fool who called me from
my sleep, encouraging the worst of my fears,
like a soothsayer. But the fool was right,
even after interrogation. I took men with me

in the night to find my daughter's groom,
threatened to burn his black heart on the end
of my silver knife, but he dismissed my threats
with his garbled music, and we all proceeded

to the Senate to learn of the Turks, but also
so I could plead my case to the Duke.
He has stolen her, I said, a girl who I might
have married off but could not bear to lose,

especially after her mother died.
Perhaps, if I am honest with myself,
it is my fault, after all, for rebuking
and deriding the suitors who came calling,

for telling them they were not adequate
for my daughter, when in fact they were
more than good enough. Had I been
wiser, there would be no grief.

The Duke is a wise man and my friend, but
I realize now he has never respected me
as a senator, only my age. Perhaps he pities me.
A widower's folly, an old man's volatility.

I railed in the Senate, disowned her, counted
her among the dead I had known and loved,
because she secretly courted the old black ram.
The thought of it now, even now, sickens me.

I did not realize the extent of my revulsion.
Or perhaps I feared that he would show her a life

too different from the one I had given her.
And in her estimation better. I am a pathetic old man.

I see that, and my heart breaks. My heart is broken.

I watch them now from the parapet that rises
above the waters that serve as streets for our city,
study them on the planks before they board
their separate ships, him clutching her,

embracing her slender figure in his thick arms,
shrouding her with his cape, kissing her,
those lips overlarge for her mouth.
They do not belong together, and I must

see them relish their misfit love, watch them
flout all that I am and have given her,
prove with their bond that I am the gull,
I am the dupe. She is cunning, as was her mother,

in her own delicate way. This girl deceived me
and she will, in time, deceive him. That is what I said,
even as I clasped their hands together in the Senate
chambers, my wedding blessing a curse.

I want my curse to come true.

He boards first and is off to destroy the Turks.
She follows on the second ship,
with her handmaiden and the General's flunkey
by her side, solicitous—her new family.

And the General's lieutenant, the womanizing fop
with his silky hair, kissing her hand before boarding
the third ship. Even he would have been a better match.
Good riddance, I call from the window, but not loud

enough for anyone to hear. I know, as I say it,
that my bitterness will corrode my heart, what's left of it.
An old senator begat a daughter whom he loved
and spoiled, and she betrayed him.

When my story is written down, that must be the epilogue.

Half-Baked Theories

Secret Theory

The problem was not
that I had a secret
but that I forgot
all secrets yearn
for revelation.

Revelation feeds
a reckoning.
And reckoning,
a recalibration.

Every story, every
plot springs from
this great aquifer.

FILCHING

Emilia: What will you do with't, that you have been so earnest
To have me filch it?

Iago: But he that filches from me my good name
Robs me of that which not enriches him,
And makes me poor indeed.

Emilia: 'Tis not a year or two shows us a man:
They are all but stomachs, and we all but food;
To eat us hungerly, and when they are full,
They belch us.

He had asked me too many times
to take the handkerchief. *Filch it*, he said.
Why did he need it? But he gave no answer,
or rather he gave multiple answers,
which is his way when he actually
has no real answer. He wanted
to have it copied for me. He wanted
to see the little squirrel—
that's what he called the General's wife—
try to explain herself.
He loved the pattern of it.
He said I didn't need to know
why he wanted, only *that* he wanted,
which may have been the closest
he has come to uttering the secret of his spirit.

Indeed, he is a secretive man, bluff and genial,
but always hoards his thoughts,
hoards his yearnings, a man who prides
himself on deciphering the secret lives of others
but who does not understand his own heart.

I told him I would not filch it from my mistress,
that he was a fool for asking me to commit
a petty crime simply to satisfy his whim,
and told him, too, that I didn't believe
he really wanted the handkerchief,
that he was merely testing me to see how far
I would go to please him, to what length
I would supplicate myself to atone
for the thousand little sins he accused
me of committing against him.

He laughed, but always that edge
of contempt in his voice and his manner:
eyebrows arching, a slight pursing of his lips.
What would you do for me? he wondered aloud.
What would you not do for me?

To complicate matters, we had been
nursing an impasse in our marriage—
a series of them, in fact. Less than a year before
was a rumor that the General and I were lovers.
I blushed at the thought, and I am not sure
that my husband did not invent the scenario
by which he heard this gossip.
Drunken murmurs, soldierly joking.

I sensed when he confronted me
that he was simply testing me,
as is his custom.
He is a man who keeps a strict
and secret tally of all grudges,
all slights to his pride—
real or imagined—
every encounter fraught
with his complex and inaccessible arithmetic.

To be honest, I was not sorry for that blush.
A smidgen of malice seasons every marriage.

The General is an exotic foreigner,
and his command of our speech is
formal and eloquent, a haunting poetry,
full of hypnotic images and music.
I can understand why his young wife is smitten.
But there has been nothing between us
except courtesy and good will,
a great and generous man showing
a pleasant deference to a beloved soldier's wife.

And I have cause for my own suspicions.
My husband gone for months at a time,
on campaigns to foreign lands:
I know him, know his appetites
and the way they must be satisfied.
It would be outlandish for me to believe
he has not done so in the brothels
that travel with the men,

sanctioned by winks, by disguised subsidies,
if not with policy.

My husband is a man who partitions
his own behavior masterfully
and will not construe his indiscretions
as indiscretions, but merely the prerogative
of a veteran soldier not yet thirty.
I have made my own cautious interrogations
about his field life, but he evades them,
makes it seem as if such details
are unworthy of even his disdain.

I do not want to know.
Yet, I do.

Only a few months later,
the General selected another man
for his lieutenancy rather than my husband—
a decision my husband
was outwardly complacent about,
yet I know he seethed.

I believe he wants me to filch
the strawberry-stitched handkerchief,
a wedding gift from the General
to his young bride, so that he might balance
an inward tally, correct the arithmetic.

To help him seems a slight enough offense,
especially if the handkerchief can be copied
for my benefit and returned shortly thereafter.

Now, with the handkerchief waiting
on the stone floor of their bedchamber,
dropped after a squabble
between the General and his wife,
I pick it up. It *is* beautiful—and mysterious.
Glittering red and gold threads, the stitching
something I have never seen before.
Perhaps there is magic in the web of it,
as the General's wife,
my friend and the woman
I gladly serve on this campaign, has told me.
Perhaps I should leave it here for her to find,
or put it on her bed, folded.

But I think of the pleasure the handkerchief
will bring my husband, think of *his* eyes
glittering, and my misbehavior
for his benefit rekindling
the heat between us, uniting us
in a way we have not been
in what seems like months now.
Perhaps the handkerchief will bewitch him,
as it has the General's wife.
And I might be, through my own wit,
the beneficiary of such witchcraft.

I bend down and take it in my hand,
feel its silk and textured threading
like welts between my fingers.
I wonder, for a moment,
if there is a reckoning stitched into the silk.

I hide it in the folds of my skirt
and steal away, amazed
that such a small crime can offer
its own pleasure and expectation.

Penny-Snatching

The trouble started when my parents called me
downstairs to perform tricks for their bombed
friends, over for an impromptu party that began
on Friday and stretched until Sunday morning.

I'd been asked to do tricks before. My best one:
penny-snatching. My ambition: to become
The Guinness Book of World Records
holder for penny-snatching. At the time, it was
seventy-two pennies, attempted and caught
by a Belgian Olympic weightlifter with hands
rumored to be as large as a normal man's foot.

My personal best thus far had been thirty-two
pennies out of forty attempted. But I was young,
and the record could be achieved, assuming
continued practice and a growth spurt.

Go ahead and show them, my mother said.
Do it for them, honey. They'll love it.
My father added theatrically, *It's really*
quite daring. I hold my breath every time
he whips his arm and snatches those coins.

I prepared myself, arranging
the stacks of pennies in five uniform
columns on the plank of my forearm.
The crowd quieted, leaned forward.

I smelled the booze, the day-old perfume,
the mixed nuts and stinky cheese.
I held my breath, stilled myself.
Waiting, waiting . . .

But this time, the pennies scattered, like buckshot,
rather than dropping neatly into my palm,
nicking two people in the eye, chipping
Mr. Engler's buck teeth, and hospitalizing
Mrs. Brown, whose mouth was open at the time
of contact, laughing at a joke, my father's lips just
inches from her ear, the flirtation the very thing
that miscalibrated my concentration.

So in reality it was my father's fault, not mine.
But that was our little secret.

POETS VS. NOVELISTS

All that distilled energy. All they do
is brood, doodle, and get drunk.
No wonder poets don't age well.

Novelists know there's another
plot twist or two or ten down the road.
They aren't looking for definitive

answers, only provisional ones.
Besides, they're too busy to brood
and drink their days and nights away.

Fiction requires a grinding sensibility,
a predilection to press down hard
with consistent pressure

for extended periods of time.
Novelists know mistakes will be made;
they accept this unfortunate fact

as the cost of compromised business,
not a tragedy. They get on with it.
They settle for good enough

if it serves their purposes. Novelists are
the writers/directors/producers/editors
of small-budget films. They do everything.

Poets, they just wait for the close-up.

Dear Big Ray

After Raymond Carver's "Popular Mechanics"

This is some scary shit, man.
I love all that "dirty water" imagery at the beginning
and the way "it was getting dark on the inside too."
Very cinematic, but also *très* symbolic.
(But is it perhaps too symbolic? Just asking.)

The wife is quite the harridan, don't you think?
All that screeching about being so glad he's leaving,
so glad he's leaving, when of course she's not glad at all.
You really made me feel her bitchery.

I'm sort of baffled, though, by how little the story's
fleshed out. This isn't even 500 words.
I thought we berated you thoroughly last workshop
on this "leaving too much out" business.
There aren't even any quotation marks!

I know your due date for workshop was the day
after we were at Lyzzard's until the wee hours of the old a.m.
If I recall clearly (always a shaky assumption),
that was the night you broke the pool cue
across that burly biker's head. (Was I dreaming,
or did he have horses tattooed on his skull?)

Anyway, I wonder if you rushed this for the deadline.
It has the feel of a hangover. (Been there, done that.)

So, back to the brevity of this piece.
The characters don't even have names!
Just a generic wife, generic husband, generic baby.
Where's the *interiority*, man? Why is he leaving?
Shouldn't we at least know *that* much?

Where's the backstory? Because I'm not inside
anyone's mind, it's hard to feel any empathy
or sympathy for this couple—
except perhaps that poor armless baby.
(Sounds like a sick joke, Big Ray.)

At least make it first person from the man's
or woman's perspective. That way I'd have
someone to root for. And, quite frankly, you're
better at first person than third.

Also, you *have* to lay off the Hemingway
stories for a while! I kept thinking that
this was what happened to the couple
in "Hills Like White Elephants"
if they decided to have a kid after all.

I longed for the blind man from that last story.
Where's the shared doobie? Where're the cathedrals?

"In this matter, the issue was decided."
Be truthful: Have you really *earned* that ending?
Seems to me that not much has been decided, has it?
Is this another attempt at irony?

Irony just does not become you, Big Ray.
You are all about earnestness.
And "Popular Mechanics"—
where did that come from?

I don't see anything popular
or mechanical in this story.
I think you've been sucking on one
too many burnt roaches, brother.
(Been there, done that.)

Suggestion alert: What about "Little Things"
as your title, especially if you're aiming
for irony? Little things *do* mean a lot.

Overall, though, I really like this draft.
Scary shit—with a *lot* of potential.
(Should I be worried about you?
Should I call Social Services?)
I just wish you'd scratch below the surface
and get to those thorny marital dynamics
you know so much about.
Remember: I only criticize because I love.

You know you rock. See you at happy hour.
4:15, Lyzzard's. You owe me a margarita
because my response is longer than your story, man.
(Who's doing the work here?)
Stay away from the pool cues and horse tattoos.

At least until I get there.

Proportions

I had entered for a while
the world of disproportion,
where I perceived the urgent
emergency of myself
as more important
than it actually was.

Our suffering always begins
with disproportion.
We must be hubbled—
humbled by the lens of the Hubble—
made aware
of our own insignificance.

Love Song from the Monterrey Aquarium Spawn Shop

Oh, let us dream now of the sea grunion,
those desperate moon riders,
scales glistening in red spume
as they rush longingly to the sand
where she can release all
four thousand in the gold crystals,
while he, driving behind her, his gills open,
his fins brushing hers, tickles the surf.

Then, without cunning or vision,
only the insistent pull of the sea
and that old grunion instinct,
he discovers her again, wraps tight
her erect-releasing dorsal,
and plunges with her, over and around,
and again too quickly
he slides down her oily scales into the sand,
the place of their own making.

They wriggle violently there.
The rip tide urges them back:
Give up this moon madness,
go back to the plankton,
back to the calm waters and moon jellies,
back to the passionless anemone.

Whereupon, exhausted, they catch
the next wave back, riding home
on their own sleepy fumes
to wait for the next full moon.

One Flesh

My wife is a cat.
Wants her space.
Plays by her rules.
Immensely pettable.
But a little aloof.
Preoccupied.
Late-night girl.
Prone to daytime naps.
Sociable but relishes
and defends her solitude.
Is this true?
Perhaps I've simply
described myself,
though in my defense,
I am allergic to cats.

Should Have Known

She should have known,
and would know next time,
if there was a next time,
never to trust a man
who does not like sex.

Such men have subterranean
resentments and grudges,
and they know how to eat
their bitterness and make it
useful for them.

Looking for Work

Don't apply for a job
you can't live without.

Don't go to an interview
if you can't say no.

Don't say no
unless you mean it.

Don't bluff your way
into a job you can't do.

Everybody in the end
hates a bullshitter.

Remember that *niche*
means two things:

The space that needs filling
and the organism filling that space.

On Receiving Three Job Rejections in Twenty-Four Hours

Today the rejections descend like hawks
into your inbox, the old wound surprising,
that you can still care enough to feel numbed
by the news you half-expected. More than half.

Yesterday, desiring to know, one way or another,
you emailed the search chairs, telling them, "Bub,
get on the stick. I've already been on one date,
and that sucker just might ask me to marry him.

If you want a shot at me, too, you better hurry
fast before someone claims me. I may be your
soul-mate. You won't know unless you find
out for yourself. Don't live in regret.

Email or call. I'm available, at your convenience,
to discuss my candidacy in greater detail,
either by phone or in person. Let's see if we're
right for each other before Contestant Number

One offers me his version of the moon. I think
your version just might be better for the both
of us. Yours, Most Humbly and Sincerely—Me."
So why are you surprised to hear back so quickly?

Virginia's correspondent tells you she was sitting
down, even as your email appeared on her screen,
with the unhappy task of informing many excellent
applicants and outstanding prospects, such as yourself,

that the vacancy has been filled, the position accepted.
And Illinois informs you, in boilerplate terms,
that you have indeed failed to cut the mustard. Texas,
most treasured prize of all, tells you the same. No go.

You didn't want those jobs anyway, did you?
You've been spared. Celebrate and give thanks.

Voice on the Page

> "First, you must enjoy the sound of your own voice.
> The trick is finding others who want to listen to it."
> —Warren Beatty

To be a writer, you must first
love to hear your own
voice on the page,
or the things you can do
with your voice,
sometimes throwing it,
like a ventriloquist,
or giving it to others,
an actor inhabiting
the scribbled body,
a conduit for spirits you
simultaneously invoke and create.

Gain control over that voice
and extend its range.
Test your talent.
A singer sings.
A painter paints.
An athlete needs a game.

Know when to let clarity
of action, image, and other
voices speak for you,
when to be

the play-by-play announcer
and when to be
the color commentator,
pure pleasure in the back and forth,
that distinctive patter.

Pollice Verso

After Jean-Léon Gérôme's *Pollice Verso*

Dear Brother,

I went again, despite
your warnings, to the contests
and was surprised by my
obsession with the fat gladiator
who sheathes his arm in golden
scales, his monstrous head filling
the bright bronze helmet with
the silver fish perched on the brim,
a leviathan swimming in the dust
of the ring, his blade a long tooth,
his arrogance sinister.

Today I watched with stupefied
horror as he felled three men.
He sliced the throat of the last
warrior, his boot on the gushing
neck, and glared at the roaring crowd
as they turned their thumbs down.

I tossed a gold medallion to him.
He caught the coin, found me,
and smiled, his tarnished teeth revealed.
He flicked his tongue lewdly.

I wanted to flee the Colosseum then,
bolt up the nut-strewn stairs.
But I could not move,
yearning for more of the fat
beast's bloody triumphs,
his dripping blade, his growing
pile of gored corpses.
I smiled back.

Strange thoughts, my brother,
a testimony and a confession.

Your loving sister,
Isabella

SPENT

I.

And he's thinking about her yet again,
about the way her head tilts back,
her long reddish-black hair tangled in her face,
a wrinkle—or is it a scar?—around her eyes.

And on the steps of the courthouse where they work,
pulling off his shoe to show her the bandage on his toe,
he says, *You know what they say about big feet, don't you?*
She looks at him quizzically. A smile lurks at the corners
of her crooked mouth, and she doesn't say a word.
He says, *Big feet, big brains.*
And she laughs, twirls away, her hair swishing.
That's not the way I heard it.
They stare at each other knowingly, teasingly.
They've been talking around the subject, testing the waters.

And then, later, another time, night.
They are outside, and it's cold, too cold
for this time of year, nearly April,
and he walks her to the car.
The street deserted, except for shadowy
figures lurking on the outskirts,
and they are talking, simply talking
to each other about something,
it doesn't matter what really,

because what they want to do
is prolong this moment in the dark,
their breaths misting, their legs bobbing
up and down on the cement to stay warm.

It seems a perfect time to do it,
to lean forward through the dark
and mist and make the connection.
He feels it like a current through him,
a wave cresting him forward,
and it takes enormous restraint to resist,
to pull back and nod as if he's been paying
attention to what she's been talking about,
which somehow relates to what almost happened
and is partly responsible for why it didn't happen.

Then she says she's not feeling well
and must go, though he knows that she knows
what almost happened, and he knows she feels it, too.
They both are afraid and clumsy.
There is a drop-off from sidewalk
to pavement, some construction work
she almost falls into, and they both laugh,
relieved, and she tells him it would be
just like her to tumble over.
I'm such a klutz, she says,
and hot fluid bubbles in his chest and head.

Click and swish and she is inside the car,
headlights on, grinding into reverse.

II.

That night in bed, his wife breathing
lightly beside him, his son and daughter
in the next rooms, he finds himself thinking
about the flutter of her tongue on his,
her lips, cracked but tender . . .
and he's not tasted them.
He finds himself wishing
he could brush against her back,
somehow possess that twirl,
be the cotton sweater she wears,
the thick jeans warming, warming.

And he wonders if this is how it will always be—
fearful and tantalizing, ticklish like the region
he imagines between her hip and hair,
neither of them willing to commit,
locked instead in this adolescent
game of anxious flirting.

Though consequences have never been his strong suit,
he also wonders what it would mean,
what toll it might exact from him.
He wonders what he will lose and if it's worth it,
if the exchange value is fair. More than fair.
He sees the whole thing exploding in his face.
His belongings on the doorstep,
nights spent alone with the television in hotels
that he can't afford, the bewildered weekends
with his son and daughter, him failing to justify

or even explain what he has done to himself or them,
having to discard his history and accept
the inevitable diminishing of his life.

For what?

For something that, once bought, can never be returned.
Once lost, never regained. Something only special
because of what it is now: unspoken potential,
simple energy, unsullied by use like a million bucks
he doesn't want to part with because what he buys
will never be worth it,
will never equal his power to spend.

He nuzzles his wife, spooning her warm
soft body, his mouth at the nape of her neck,
and he's trying to drift off, let it pass,
as these things will. A trick of the heart.
He shuts his eyes. But, almost against his will,
he's thinking about her yet again,
about the way her head tilts back,
her long reddish-black hair tangled in her face,
a wrinkle—or is it a scar?—around her eyes.

She is there, just beyond reach, and he holds
the image in his mind, holds it as long as he can
before sleep takes her away.

Smitten

Bianca: O my dear Cassio! my sweet Cassio! O Cassio, Cassio, Cassio!

Cassio: This is the monkey's own giving out: she is persuaded I will marry her, out of her own love . . .

Bianca: I am no strumpet; but of life as honest As you that thus abuse me.

He came to my bed with money, but by the end,
it was me who was smitten, me who longed
for his return, me who sought *him* out.

This was in Cyprus, where I traveled,
along with the other women,
to be with the soldiers, a separate
ship paid by the Senate.

Sent as reward for reclaiming the island,
even though the Turks had drowned
because of the wind and sea,
not because of Venetian courage.

But who was I to complain? Satisfied men,
steady work, island beauty.

He had just arrived, the General's lieutenant,
a Florentine, trim and slender,
an impeccably dressed officer
with thick black hair and feline grace.

I felt the thrumming then, though it was financial
as much as, if not more than, sexual desire,
the two frequently entwined for me.

I was not happy about the handkerchief—
the one with strawberries—some lewd
minx's token he wanted copied.
I would not duplicate another woman's
stitching as a gift for myself. An insult!

I saw him last as I left the isle, not long after
the tragedy with the General and his wife,
not long after I myself was exonerated.

He came to my bed, our final lust tinged
with melancholy and elegy and the pain
in his wounded thigh when we grew too ardent.

The clumsy lovemaking of last things. After that,
I did not want him, not in the same
needful way. I was relieved to have
my yearning weakened.

Unhappy, though, that he would not be a new
fate for me. I soon left for another outpost,
where the soldiers were plentiful
and in need of companionship.

I have not seen him in many years. I hear
he is the Governor of Cyprus, has married
and has many sons and daughters,
has grown fat and complacent and cautious.

This is what men do. I do not know why
I thought he might be any different.

PROGNOSTICATION

If suffering is the great
wellspring of art,
then is grief
the only tale
in this darkness?

Not wanting the world
to go its carnivorous way,
blithely eating time,
do we simply rage
over losing what we love?

Or do we give voice
to what we've lost,
so we will understand
who we have become,
the artists we might be?

Notes and Acknowledgments

"Her First Husband": Macbeth is haunted by his and Lady Macbeth's childlessness, which he blames on his "barren scepter," yet Lady Macbeth says that she has breastfed her own children; this poem supposes that she had an earlier marriage. I have, in the third epigraph of this poem, intentionally changed "gripe" to "grip" for clarity.

"Hail Mary": The game-winning touchdown referenced here is the original Hail Mary pass, so named after Roger Staubach said, in a post-game interview, "I closed my eyes and said a Hail Mary."

"Postcard from the Chauncey Griggs House in Tacoma": The Chauncey Griggs House was built by Frank Lloyd Wright in 1946. Olgivanna was Wright's second wife. Wright's mistress, her children, and other servants were killed at Wright's first Taliesin home in Wisconsin when a servant set fire to the house and then stood in the doorway and murdered everyone as they tried to escape through the only doorway, an idiosyncratic architectural feature that Wright insisted on early in his career.

"January at MacDowell": The MacDowell Colony, in Peterborough, New Hampshire, is one of the oldest artist colonies in the world. Thorton Wilder, a frequent resident at MacDowell, based Grover's Corners, his fictional community in *Our Town*, on Peterborough.

"The Senator's Dream": In *Othello*, Brabantio, a Venetian senator, is first alerted to the news of his daughter Desdemona's secret marriage to Othello by Iago and Rodrigo, who awake him from a portentous dream. After the senator curses the couple's marriage, he is not referenced again until the end of the play, when news arrives that he died from grief caused by his daughter's betrayal.

"Filching": In *Othello*, Emilia steals Desdemona's handkerchief for her husband Iago, who uses it to convince Othello of his wife's infidelity.

"Dear Big Ray": This fictional critique by a workshop buddy of Raymond Carver is in response to Carver's often anthologized tragic parable about a couple whose argument over their child escalates into a terrible tug-of-war. In his final volume of new and selected stories, *Where I'm Calling From*, Carver changed the title from "Popular Mechanics" to "Little Things."

"Looking for Work": I am indebted to Dan Bauer for interview advice and to Tim Crews, an agroecologist, for the double meaning of *niche*.

"*Pollice Verso*": This poem is inspired by French artist Jean-Léon Gérôme's 1872 painting of a triumphant gladiator being cheered by Colosseum spectators.

"Smitten": In *Othello*, Bianca is a prostitute who has fallen in love with Othello's lieutenant, Cassio. She plays an unwitting role in Iago's plot to dupe Othello and murder Cassio.

Some of these poems appeared, in different form, in *The South Dakota Review, Elsewhere, The Pinch, Gemini Magazine, Curepub,* and *Valley Guide Quarterly.*

I very much appreciate the fellowships, which aided in the writing and revision of this book, from The Arizona Commission on the Arts, Blue Mountain Center, the MacDowell Colony, the Corporation of Yaddo, and the Fairhope Center for the Writing Arts. I am also grateful for research grants from the Center for Excellence in the Arts

& Humanities, the College of Liberal Arts & Sciences, and the Faculty Professional Development Assignment Program at Iowa State University.

My thanks to these individuals: Wayne Regina, Tim Crews, Janet Bicknese, Sarah Crews, Deb Marquart, Mary Swander, Ned Balbo, and Dan Bauer, and my colleagues in Spalding University's MFA Program, at Prescott College, and at Iowa State University. Steve Semken, thank you for your support and for being a champion of Midwestern literary culture. Special thanks to my sister Brandy and my children—Lena and Vivian (whose faces are hidden behind the masks on the cover), Tristan, and Carson.

I am grateful to Sheila Sanderson, Joe Schuster, and especially my wife Charissa Menefee for their insights and detailed comments on drafts of this book.